★ TODAY'S ★
HEROES

Dave
Dravecky

Other Books in the Today's Heroes Series

★ TODAY'S ★
HEROES

Dave
Dravecky

Gregg & Deborah Shaw Lewis

Zonderkidz

Zonder**kidz**™

The children's group of Zondervan

www.zonderkidz.com

Today's Heroes: Dave Dravecky
Copyright © 2002 by Gregg and Deborah Shaw Lewis

Requests for information should be addressed to:
Grand Rapids, Michigan 49530

ISBN: 0-310-70314-X

Dave Dravecky may be contacted at Dave Dravecky's Outreach of Hope, 13840 Gleneagle Drive, Colorado Springs, CO 80921, www.OutreachOfHope.org

Editor: Barbara J. Scott
Interior design: Todd Sprague
Art direction: Michelle Lenger
Printed in the United States of America

02 03 04 05 06 07/❖DC/ 10 9 8 7 6 5 4 3 2 1

CONTENTS

1

THE BEGINNING OF THE DREAM

Every day, Mr. Dravecky would come home from work smelling of sweat and grease from his machine shop, his trousers smeared with the day's work, and his fingernails black with grime. His young son Dave used to look at his dad washing the grease from his hands and think, *Such big hands. Such big, strong hands.*

"As a kid growing up," Dave says, "I felt safe and secure knowing those fix-anything hands belonged to the man I called Dad. And no matter how tired those hands were at the end of the day, they were never too tired for a game of catch with me. In the backyard my dad would burrow one of those big hands into a catcher's mitt and play with a seven-year-old boy who could barely wrap his hand around a baseball. I remember how he would crouch down and pound his fist into that mitt, making a well-rounded pocket for the ball I was about to pitch. Often we played until it was too dark to see, and still I begged for more, never wanting that time to end."

And that's where Dave Dravecky's dream began, when he was a young boy, pitching to his father in their family's backyard.

It wasn't long until the Dravecky backyard became a ball diamond where all the neighborhood kids would come to play. They wore base paths between the trees used for bases, hit foul balls that ricocheted off the house, and knocked homers over and past the fenceless yards of neighbors.

"The backyard was never the same after the first time my dad put on that glove and played catch with me," Dave says, "and neither was I."

2

LET'S PLAY BALL!

Dave's fascination with baseball came as no surprise to his parents. The first word his mother ever heard him say was "ball."

On cold, snowy, Ohio winter days, young Dave would spend hours sitting on the family room floor, bouncing a tennis ball off the brick fireplace, waiting for spring to come so he could be playing baseball outside. Once spring finally did arrive and the snow began to melt, Dave would carry a baseball in a glove tucked under his arm everywhere he went—in hopes of scaring up a game with friends.

Those endless backyard and sandlot games with neighborhood friends and brothers continued long after they all moved up to organized ball.

Little League. Pony League. Colt League. Dave played and loved them all. His younger brothers, Rick, Frankie, and Joey, played with him, and their dad often helped coach those teams.

Baseball played a big part in the Dravecky family life. If they weren't playing it, they were huddled around the black and white television set in the family room, rooting for the Cleveland Indians. Sometimes Dave's Uncle Andy, who played in the minor leagues for the Pittsburgh Pirates, would drop by and watch with them. Baseball seemed to be in the Dravecky blood.

Evidently there was more than a little mischief in that clan as well. Those boys could be trouble. One time, Mr. and Mrs. Dravecky hired a baby-sitter to watch their four sons while the couple went out for the evening. Dave was around ten years old, so his brother Ricky must have been nine, Frankie about seven, and Joey six. The four of them banded together to find the answer to one question: What can we do to drive this girl crazy?

Their answer: strip off all their clothes and run screaming from room to room. The baby-sitter didn't know what to do with four naked little boys running around the house. But when they opened the door and raced outside, she really panicked, chasing them around the yard while the Dravecky boys all scattered and ran and laughed like crazy. They had shown her! (In more ways than one.) They had also succeeded in getting into trouble with their parents because that poor girl never agreed to baby-sit for them again.

Dave and his brothers were a real handful. They fought among themselves sometimes, as brothers often do. But any neighborhood kid knew that if he went against one Dravecky, he had better be ready to take on the rest.

One day Frankie got into a fight in a yard across the street from the Dravecky house. Ricky saw the commotion and ran across to take up for his younger brother. When Ricky jumped into the fight, he ended up breaking the other boy's arm. He felt sorry about it later, but he couldn't let someone beat up his brother.

Another time, when Dave was in first or second grade, he and a friend got into a kick fight while waiting for their ride home from school. They were just messing around, not really trying to hurt each other. But when the older brother of Dave's friend saw them, he came running over to protect *his* little brother. He grabbed Dave by the back of his hair and pushed his face into a brick wall. Dave ended up with a chipped tooth.

Loyalty to brothers was just a part of growing up in Boardman, Ohio. And Boardman, a suburb of Youngstown, is where David and his brothers grew up—in the same house their parents still own today. The backyard of their home bordered

Mill Creek Park. That's where the Dravecky boys hiked in the woods and built forts, where they climbed trees and sat in the upper branches talking with friends for hours at a time.

In the winter the boys would scramble across a log over an icy creek, with their skates around their necks, and hike to a frozen pond to play hockey. "The boys" included not only the Draveckys, but also as many as twenty-five guys from their neighborhood who were all good buds.

Dave remembers riding his bike with a pack of friends, making the seventeen-mile run through Mill Creek Park from the neighborhood where they lived to the farthest edge of the park, all the way to Youngstown, and then back home. The same group of boys played countless football and baseball games together. Summer and winter, spring and fall, they would stay outside until they heard their dinner bells ringing or their mothers calling them home for supper.

Except on frigid winter days, the only time Dave spent inside his house (aside from sleeping) was on Saturday morning when he would watch cartoons and eat a box of cereal for breakfast. Then, when he would hear his friends begin to gather outside, Dave would head out and play ball for the rest of the day.

One of Dave's good friends was a boy named Mike Berezo. Both good baseball players, Dave and Mike played on opposing Little League teams. One day, when Dave was eleven or twelve years old, their teams went head-to-head. Dave was pitching and still had a no-hitter going late in the game when Mike came up to bat. It was friend against friend. Dave knew, from playing with him in the neighborhood, how well Mike could hit. He also knew that Mike was well aware of what Dave could throw. Could he beat him here, in Little League, with the crowd watching and cheering? Or would Mike end his no-hitter?

Dave took a deep breath and let go with his best pitch. Mike ripped the ball—straight at the shortstop. But the ball skipped through the infielder's legs and Mike ended up safe at first.

Dave did go on and set down all the other hitters he faced that day, and the game ended with his team winning. The scorekeeper ruled Mike's at bat as an error, not a hit. The two friends spent the next few months arguing over whether Mike got a hit or Dave earned a no-hitter.

It seemed as if Dave and his brothers spent all their time playing ball and getting into fights. Maybe that was one reason Dave's parents felt it was important to bring their children up in the teachings of the Catholic Church. The family all attended mass every Sunday.

Dave served as an altar boy in his church for years. He would light candles in the sanctuary and hold the cup while the priest served Communion. And when the service ended, he would put the leftover wafers and the wine away for the priest. He listened to what the priest had to say every Sunday and could recite the entire mass in Latin. "I grew up loving God and understanding church was a holy place," Dave says. "I even remember a specific time after the service one Sunday when I really sensed that God loved me and was going to do something special in my life."

Dave and his brothers received additional religious training during the week at their parish elementary school, St. Charles. He enjoyed school and made good grades. Of course the part of school Dave liked best was recess—when he could play ball with his friends.

As a rule, Dave would carry a ball of one kind or another wherever he went, just in case a game broke out. One day, when he started misbehaving in class, the teacher corrected him. This teacher was a nun who, when Dave talked back to her, walked over to his desk and took his basketball. Dave got mad. How dare she take his property— that basketball was his. She couldn't just take it away! But she did, and when Dave told her she couldn't, he ended up in the principal's office.

Most of the time the teachers and staff of St. Charles were happy about Dave's attachment to all kinds of balls because he was a regular star on the school sports teams. Not only did he continue to play baseball, but he took up basketball and football as well. In fact his first big experience with athletic stardom came on the gridiron. Dave ran the ball for his eighth-grade football team, which stood undefeated for the season and ended up playing for the championship. It was St. Charles versus St. Patrick's. Big cross-town rivals. Each undefeated. Parish against parish. People all over town were talking about the big game.

The game lived up to its billing. For a long time it looked like the bruising, hard-fought contest was going to end in a 0–0 tie. But late in the game, St. Charles drove the ball to within a foot of the end zone. Fourth down. Time ticking off. The coach called, "Thirty-two dive"—a fullback run. Dave was the fullback. He took the handoff from his quarterback, plowed into a mass of players at the line of scrimmage, and crashed to the ground.

Under the pile, realizing he'd fallen right on the goal line, Dave nudged the ball forward and just lay there. When the refs finally pulled every-one off of him, they signaled a touchdown.

St. Charles beat St. Pats. Dave Dravecky was the hero of the entire parish.

3

DRAFTED!

Football was king of high school sports in that part of Ohio. So Dave's reputation as a young athlete, particularly his success in junior high football, attracted the attention of coaches and fans at his town's Catholic high school. They were anxious to see the Dravecky kid running the ball out of the backfield for their football team. Instead, because the Catholic school didn't have a baseball team, Dave opted to attend public school at nearby Boardman High.

Boardman's football coach was glad to learn that Dave had enrolled in his school. But when Dave told him he also wanted to play baseball, the coach told him he couldn't play two sports and still give football his best effort. Dave said that was fine, he'd play baseball. It wasn't a difficult choice. He liked football, but not the way he loved and lived baseball.

The Boardman basketball coach didn't have the same one-sport rule as the football coach, so Dave played high-school round ball in the winter and baseball in the spring throughout his high school years. He was a well-rounded athlete, but it soon became obvious that Dave Dravecky would make the biggest impact on the baseball field. Left-handed pitchers are always at a premium, and he was clearly a good one.

One summer when he was fourteen or fifteen, Dave's dad took him to Cleveland to see a major-league baseball game. Watching a young, little-known Indian pitcher by the name of Dennis Eckersley warm up in the Cleveland bullpen, Frank Dravecky turned to his son and asked, "Think you could do that someday?"

Without hesitating, Dave told his father, "Yeah! I could do that."

But those words were more a declaration of hope than they were a reflection of reasoned confidence or even youthful cockiness. Reflecting back on that time, Dave says, "I certainly had some talent, and I definitely dreamed about someday playing college or professional ball. But I wasn't always that confident about my personal abilities. Yes, I was considered a good player in

Youngstown, Ohio. But I couldn't help wondering if there weren't a lot of other kids my age in Florida, Texas, or California who might be a whole lot better."

With great hope of finding out how he would measure up against those kids someday, Dave admits that he invested a lot more in athletics than he did in academics during high school. He wasn't a bad student, but he was never as concerned about test scores in the classroom as he was final scores out on the baseball diamond. As long as he made good enough grades to get into college and play baseball at the next level, he was happy.

Dave learned some of his most important lessons, not in the schoolroom or even on the playing field, but in the arena of life. One such lesson was learned when Dave and his brother Ricky planned a weekend outing with a few of their friends. This camping trip wasn't scheduled as much to enjoy the outdoors as it was for the boys to get away by themselves and to stir up a little trouble, which included drinking alcohol.

The whole thing got off to a less-than-wonderful start as Dave drove back through the woods to get to their campsite. The car fishtailed and skidded a little on the dirt trail and clipped a nearby tree—leaving a noticeable dent in the back quarter panel of his dad's station wagon. When

Dave got out to survey the damage he thought, *These things happen. Dad will understand.*

But they still hadn't reached their destination when a low-hanging branch caught the car's antenna and snapped it right off. *We can replace an antenna easy enough,* Dave assured himself. *That won't be very expensive.* But after they set up their tents, Dave and his buddies thought the open field next to their campsite would be perfect for a little harmless stunt driving. So Dave revved up the engine of the station wagon and spun a few donuts in the grass—grass just tall enough to keep him from spotting the stump which, when he ran over it, knocked the entire muffler off the car. For the rest of that trip, Dave tried not to think about what his father was going to say when he got home. Sitting around the campfire that evening, the boys drank what beer and wine they'd managed to bring along.

But when Dave and Ricky got home, they decided they would be less conspicuous if they parked the mufflerless car out on the street, rather than pull into the driveway and up to the garage near to where their folks were hosting a backyard picnic for friends. But they no sooner had shut off the roaring engine than their father came walking around the house to investigate the noise. He took one look at his station wagon and ordered both boys, "Get in the house. Now!"

Mr. Dravecky came in and confronted them a few minutes later to find out what in the world had happened. Dave matter-of-factly explained how each of the three "accidents" had occurred. His father listened, and Dave breathed a sigh of relief when his dad calmly nodded and said he could understand how any of those things could happen.

But then he said, "Tell me one other thing now. Were you boys drinking?"

Dave looked at Ricky, who was obviously wanting, and waiting for, his big brother to lie. Instead Dave looked right at his father and told him, "Yes, sir, we were."

Ricky stared at his brother in disbelief as if to say, *How could you tell him that?* He looked as if he wanted to take Dave's head off.

Dave explains, "I made an instant decision that I'd be better off telling the truth than having Dad find out I lied. And I was right. My father told me he really appreciated the fact that I'd been honest enough to confess the truth. Our punishment was being grounded for the rest of the weekend. But he told us not to worry about the car, the damage wasn't serious, and he was more concerned that we had learned our lesson from the experience. I certainly learned the value of telling the truth."

That experience and others during his first couple of years in high school also helped teach

Dave the value of choosing his friends wisely. He was involved for a time with a number of guys, several of whom he'd grown up with, who were making some very poor choices, including drinking and taking drugs. As a teenager, Dave was no longer very excited about having to attend catechism class and church every week; he went because his folks expected him to. He wasn't interested when people would invite him to Christian events and programs like the Fellowship of Christian Athletes. Spiritual things just didn't hold any appeal.

However, his parents and the time he spent in church had instilled in Dave a strong sense of right and wrong. He knew that taking drugs was wrong, and he didn't want to get involved with them. Yet every weekend it seemed that friends would offer him drugs. Several of those friends began to smoke pot, and eventually took cocaine, making it part of their before-school routine. Dave got so fed up with their attempts to recruit him that he told them in no uncertain terms never to offer drugs to him again. He also made a deliberate effort to spend more of his time with new friends. Since so much of his life was focused on sports, he decided to hang around other athletes who weren't doing drugs. His new set of friends reduced the peer pressure he'd been feeling before.

Another major influence on his life during high school was a girl he met at a local mall during his sophomore year. Janice Roh went to a rival high school across town and was dating a good friend of Dave's. "As soon as they broke up," Dave says, "I jumped right in and asked her out." It wasn't long before he decided his dreams for the future included baseball *and* Jan.

Unfortunately, baseball after high school didn't look promising. Despite Dave's fairly successful high school pitching career, no college baseball program showed the least bit of interest in him. Dave didn't receive a single college scholarship, not even from a local junior college. Sensing how discouraged his left-handed pitcher was, Boardman High's baseball coach, whom Dave greatly respected, called him into his office one day. The coach told Dave, "I really think you have the ability to play at the next level. You need to continue in baseball even if you have to walk on somewhere and earn a spot."

With his coach's encouragement, that's what Dave determined to do. So he and Jan decided they would go off to the University of Ohio together. When their parents discouraged that idea, they decided to stay home and commute together to nearby Youngstown State University. After all, YSU had a baseball program. In time, Dave would become an important part of it.

By his junior year Dave so wanted to become a major-league pitcher that he became consumed by baseball. His win-loss record that year was 7–1 with a practically microscopic 0.88 earned-run average. The strength of his pitching helped Youngstown State to the NCAA Division II baseball tournament for the first time in school history. YSU head coach Dom Roselli handed Dave the game ball before the opening game against Wright State and told him, "Go get 'em!" Dave walked to the mound confidently, ready to show his stuff not only to Wright State, but also to the two dozen major-league scouts in the stands that day. He wanted to prove once and for all that he could be the next Sandy Koufax.

Instead, every pitch he threw rocketed off a bat for a single, a double, or a home run. His coach finally sent him to the showers in the third inning after he'd given up nine runs—eight of them earned. Dave hung his head on the long walk to the dugout. He knew no scouts would want to talk to him after the game that YSU eventually lost 26–1.

Dave thought about his performance, trying to figure out why things had gone so wrong. Then it hit him: He'd forgotten the advice his father had always given him. Time and again Mr. Dravecky had told his son two things that he believed applied both to sports and life: "Whatever you do, work hard at it. Don't shortchange yourself; be the best you can be. But more important, go out and have fun."

In his drive to succeed, Dave had forgotten the fun part. Dave put himself under tremendous pressure trying so hard to impress the scouts that all the joy was gone from the game, and as a result, he performed poorly. So Dave approached his senior year of college baseball with a different attitude. He says, "Since I didn't think I was going anywhere, I played baseball for the game's sake. I had a blast all year long." He had only a 3–2 record that spring, but near the end of the season he pitched a three-hit, seven-inning shutout against Clarion State in which he struck out fourteen hitters. There happened to be a Pirates scout at that game, and Dave received an invitation to a one-day tryout camp at Three Rivers Stadium in Pittsburgh.

The tryout went well. Dave got a thrill playing in a big-league ballpark for the very first time, throwing one perfect inning in a scrimmage game against other guys who'd been invited to try out. That was it. At the end of the workout, when he asked the Pirates' farm director what happened next, the man told Dave to go home and sit by the phone. "If someone calls," he said, "you've been drafted. If you aren't called, you'll have to find something else to do with your life."

On the second day of baseball's amateur draft that June, the whole family hung around the Dravecky house. No one was allowed to use the phone. When it finally rang, Rick answered, listened for a minute, and then handed the receiver to Dave. "It's for you," he whispered. "I think this is it."

The voice on the phone said, "Dave, this is Murray Cook of the Pittsburgh Pirates. We've just selected you as our twenty-first pick in the summer draft. We're shipping you to our minor-league team in Charleston, South Carolina. We've just signed another fellow from Butler, Pennsylvania, and we're trying to make arrangements for him to swing by and take you to Charleston."

Only after he hung up the phone did Dave begin screaming, "I got drafted! I got drafted!"

Maybe the dream would come true.

4

PLAYING IN THE MINORS

Wow! Dave thought as it all began to sink in. *I'm finally going to be a professional baseball player.* But that's not the same thing as being a big-league baseball player. He would spend the next several years learning how different it was, how far he'd have to go to make it to the majors, and how few players ever reach that goal.

The Pittsburgh Pirates weren't expecting a lot from a twenty-first round draft pick, so they didn't invest much. Other players received signing bonuses and incentive clauses promising to pay them more if they played well, but Dave got neither. The Pirates offered Dave just $500 a month to play that season for their Class A team in Charleston, South Carolina. Dave didn't care.

He probably would have played for nothing—nothing but the chance to continue his baseball career. He pitched in twenty games that year, mostly in relief, and ended the season with a 4–2 record. He hadn't played great, but he did well enough that when he and Jan got married that fall of 1978, he knew he would be pitching in the Pirates' organization again the next season.

The Pirates moved Dave up to their Class AA team in Buffalo for the 1979 season. That meant he was one step closer to his dream of playing in the majors. Double-A baseball wasn't glamorous. The crowds were small and most of the stadiums old and run-down. The ballpark in Buffalo was crawling with rats that feasted on popcorn, peanuts, and Crackerjacks beneath the stands. Dave chalked up six wins against seven losses that year and wasn't sure if that would be good enough to be invited back the following season. So when the Pirates' organization suggested he go to Colombia to play that fall, Dave wasn't about to argue. For a young married couple, the idea of playing in South America sounded like an adventure. And it was. Even though it didn't end the way they'd pictured.

The Pirates assigned Dave to a team in Barranquilla, Colombia—a city on the country's Caribbean coast. He and Jan pictured a tropical paradise. But when they got there, Barranquilla turned out to be a hot, sticky, filthy, industrial town with open sewers, incredible poverty, and cockroaches as big as mice. Dave played so poorly the fans would throw corncobs at him on the field. In the stands, when they figured out she was his wife, fans would hiss at Jan and make signs with their hands like they were pointing a gun at her head. Things went from bad to worse when Dave got sick with a 104-degree fever and lost fifteen pounds in five days. For the first time in his life, Dave desperately called out to God for help.

When he finally recovered enough to try to pitch again, he was so weak he could put nothing on the ball. The team released him and Dave felt like the luckiest guy in the world. He and Jan would be able to leave Colombia and be back home in Ohio for the holidays. Back in the States, Dave promised Jan they would never go back to Colombia again. When he posted a 13–7 record in Buffalo during the 1980 season, he felt certain the Pirates would move him up to Triple-A the following year. But he knew he still had a lot to prove because there were people in the Pirates' organization who didn't think he was a true major-league prospect. So when it was suggested that Dave play another season of winter ball in Colombia, he told them he'd do it.

Jan wasn't happy. She understood Dave's position, but her memories of Colombia were so bad she didn't think she could take another season down there. So she accepted a good job with an accounting firm in Florida to earn them some much needed money; Dave still only made $600 to $700 a month while he was playing. Dave headed to South America again, where he stayed in the same horrible apartment he and Jan had lived in the year before. He missed his wife so much and played so poorly that the Barranquilla team released him yet again.

As thrilled as he was to rejoin Jan in Sarasota, as determined as he was never to let baseball or anything else separate him from his wife again, Dave also now had some serious doubts about his future. He was convinced he'd reached the do-or-die stage of his career. If he didn't make the jump to Triple-A the next season, he figured the Pirates would trade him to another club, or more likely, release him and bring his baseball dream to a sudden and disappointing end.

Sure enough, near the end of spring training, the director of the Pirates' farm system, Murray Cook, called for Dave in the clubhouse. "We've traded you," he said.

Realizing that wasn't necessarily bad news, a thought flashed through Dave's mind, *I hope it's to San Diego.* Just a few days before a bunch of players had been talking about the best club to play for, and they'd all pretty much agreed on San

Diego. It was a young, improving team that played in a great city with a wonderful climate. Plus, their Triple-A team was in Hawaii—where better to play in the minors? *Say I've been traded to San Diego and I need to report to Hawaii!*

"We've traded you to San Diego, Dave," Cook told him. *Wonderful!* Dave thought. "You're heading to Amarillo." *Where?*

Amarillo was another Double-A team. However, West Texas was about as far from Hawaii as you could get—blistering hot, windy, dusty, flat, and dull. But at least Dave was playing for a new club with a new chance to prove himself.

Jan stayed in Florida for a few weeks to earn the money they would need to live on during the coming year. Dave headed to Texas and checked into the Holiday Inn where all the ballplayers were staying until they found other accommodations. Sharing Dave's room was a tall, redheaded, freckle-faced ballplayer with size-fifteen feet. Everyone liked Byron Ballard. He had a zany sense of humor and obviously enjoyed life. Dave noticed some Christian books on Byron's bed and commented on them.

Byron asked if Dave knew about baseball chapel, a brief voluntary prayer and worship service for players and coaches held before the game every Sunday in minor-league and major-league ballparks.

"Sure," Dave told his roommate, "I was a chapel leader in Buffalo."

Byron's eyes lit up. He immediately assumed that Dave was a born-again Christian. So Dave quickly tried to straighten him out. He told Byron that he'd grown up in a religious home and always had a respect for God. In times of trouble he prayed, and he went to church on Sundays whenever he could. "I'm sorry," he said, "but I really don't understand that born-again stuff."

That wasn't their last discussion on the subject. During the next few weeks they had many discussions. Byron explained what "born again" meant; he even got out his Bible and showed Dave where Jesus talked about it in John 3:3. Dave was impressed. This guy obviously knew something. Byron didn't try to argue or push his beliefs on Dave. He let Dave ask the questions and then helped him find the answers in the Bible.

Dave considered himself a Christian. He grew up believing there was a God, but God had always seemed distant and impersonal. You respected him, but you didn't really know him. He'd never actually read the Bible. In fact, when they were first married, Jan had suggested they try reading it together. Dave told her, "I can never read that, Janice. I just don't understand it. That's for priests to read, not me."

With Byron's help, Dave began to see that the Bible had plenty to say that he could understand, things that turned his ideas about God upside down. God wasn't distant and vague. He wanted to be close to people so much that he came to earth in the form of a man, Jesus, to die for each one of us. Dave had always believed that he was basically a good person. He didn't understand why Byron thought he was a sinner. So Byron showed him where the Bible says, in Romans 3:23, that all human beings are sinners because they all mess up. No one can measure up to all that God intended them to be and do. Dave was amazed that no one had explained this to him before—how sin kept him from having a close relationship to God.

Then Dave asked the question: How do people get rid of their sin and begin to relate to God? Byron again showed him places in the Bible that talked about the need to confess sins and ask for God's forgiveness. One of the verses that really struck Dave and stuck with him was Romans 10:9. It says, "If you confess with your mouth, 'Jesus is Lord,' and believe in your heart that God raised him from the dead, you will be saved."

It sounded so plain, so simple—maybe too simple. Dave didn't come to believe in Christ overnight. Instead, he watched Byron like a hawk, trying to figure him out. When Jan finally got to Amarillo, she was afraid her husband was turning into a religious nut because all Dave wanted to talk to her about was what he was reading in and learning from the Bible. In time, after talking with other people, reading Christian books, and studying the Bible, Jan began sorting through her own questions.

Dave and Jan eventually agreed that if God is as personal as Byron and the Bible said, their lives would have to change. If God cared about every detail of their lives, then he knew what was best for them. So they both made the decision to commit themselves to trust the personal, loving God they had learned about in the Bible and to follow Jesus wherever he might lead them.

In some ways, playing in Amarillo was as bad as everyone had said it would be with the heat, wind, dust, and a plague of flies from the stockyards next to the stadium. Some days the smell got so bad the players didn't want to breathe. Yet for Dave and Jan that season became one of the most important and wonderful years of their lives. They were so broke they shared an apartment with a single guy just to afford the rent. Yet several of the Amarillo players and their wives were new Christians, and they were all excited about learning together. The whole group attended the same church and spent hours reading and discussing the Bible. Many of those people became the Draveckys' lifelong friends.

Amarillo may have been the last place on earth Dave had wanted to go that summer of 1981, but he now says, "I wouldn't trade the hours we spent together there for time in any locker room on the face of the earth."

Dave not only grew spiritually in Texas, he had his best year yet in baseball. Used mostly as a starter, he won fifteen games while losing only five, and he lowered his ERA (Earned Run Average) to just 2.67 runs allowed per game. The Padres named him their minor-league Player of the Year and promoted him to their Hawaii team to start the 1982 season.

That was a huge jump for Dave. Double-A teams travel on buses to play in dingy stadiums in small towns. Triple-A teams usually fly and play in big cities. All players dream of making it to the majors someday, and in Triple-A, you know that you're just one phone call away from the big league. "You felt it," Dave says. "You were right on the verge of fulfilling your lifelong dream."

5

CALLED TO THE MAJORS

Many of the Draveckys' friends from Amarillo moved to Hawaii with them. A few—Andy and Jackie Hawkins, Mark and Debbie Thurmond, Tony and Alicia Gwynn—would make the big leagues with them. Others—the Gausepohls, the DeSimones, the Merediths, and the Smiths—didn't get the same breaks. "But at that time," Dave remembers, "we were all scrambling together, full of hope and having the time of our lives."

Tony Gwynn, who went on to have a Hall of Fame career with the Padres, started out in Amarillo with "the worst throwing mechanics" Dave says he'd ever seen. His outfield throws were "limp balloons." Dave says, "Never have I seen someone work as hard as he did to improve.

Of course, Tony had tremendous raw ability but he wouldn't have become great without incredible work."

Jan was seven months pregnant with the Draveckys' first baby when they moved to Hawaii in 1982. While he was in Phoenix on a two-week road trip, Jan called Dave in a panic. It was the middle of the night, the baby was about to come, and she had to leave for the hospital. Dave caught an early morning flight that landed in Honolulu at 11:30 A.M. At 11:39 A.M., while he was still en route to the hospital, Jan gave birth to a beautiful and healthy little girl they named Tiffany. As bad as he felt about not being there with Jan during her labor, Dave was thrilled that his team was going back to Honolulu for a twenty-game home stand. He'd try to make up for missing his daughter's birth by spending lots of time together with Jan and Tiffany for the next three weeks.

But two days after Tiffany's birth, just as he was walking out of the apartment to head to the hospital, the phone rang. It was Bob Cluck, the Padres' farm director. He asked about Jan and congratulated Dave on becoming a father. Dave was pleasantly surprised by the gesture. He thought, *Hey, that's nice. These people really care.* Then Mr. Cluck told him, "There's actually another reason why I called. We're calling you up. You're coming to the big leagues."

Dave thought he was joking, and it took several minutes before he was convinced. He'd spent five years in the minors. It had taken three years to finally get from Double-A to Triple-A. Now just ten weeks into the season he was getting The Call.

As soon as he hung up, Dave phoned the hospital to tell Jan. When she started crying, Dave thought she was happy. Then he realized she was upset about him leaving her to say good-bye to friends, pack all their stuff, move out of the apartment, sell their car, and move across the ocean with a baby less than a week old. Jan and Tiffany got out of the hospital early so the Draveckys could spend a day together. The next morning Dave kissed them both good-bye and flew to California.

By the time she and Tiffany joined him a few days later, Jan could tell something was wrong. Dave wasn't eating or communicating. When she asked what the problem was, he said everything was fine. When she asked if he was feeling pressured and nervous he said no. But Dave pitched terribly and didn't have a clue why. The more he pitched, the more discouraged he got and the worse he'd pitch. "It's a dreadful thing to build your life on a goal and then sense that you're failing," he says.

He couldn't concentrate. He couldn't think. Then the pitching coach told him in as nice a way as he could what Dave already knew in his heart, "You've got to throw strikes, Dave, or they're going to send you back to Hawaii." So the pressure continued to build. Coaches and friends had lots of advice for Dave. He couldn't tell them he was scared. He couldn't tell anyone.

Finally, after three weeks or so, as he was getting ready to leave for a game against the Dodgers, Jan tried again. "I know something is wrong, David," she told him. "What is it?"

Tired of carrying the load all by himself, Dave broke down and told her what the pitching coach had said about needing to throw strikes.

"Well, David," Jan said sweetly, "why can't you throw strikes?"

So he told her everything. He said he didn't have any idea where he was throwing the ball, and when he stood on the mound, he started thinking about being in the big leagues and how all the guys he was facing were big-league hitters. He told her how he heard everything the crowd was saying and couldn't concentrate. "I get the heebie-jeebies," Dave said. "I'm scared, Janice."

Jan began to cry. She shed tears for Dave, but also because he'd never opened up and shared his deepest feelings with her before. They held each other and talked. Mostly Jan talked.

"What are you afraid of?" she asked. "All you can do is your best. If that's not good enough, so what? What's the worst that could happen? We'll be sent back to Hawaii! I'd love to go. I liked it better there. I was having a blast. We'd be with all our friends again. I'd be thrilled."

Dave realized she was right. Even if he failed, he wasn't going to lose the things that mattered most. His wife. Their baby daughter. Friends.

"You're forgetting what you've always said," Jan added. "Remember? You and Byron used to say that you should pitch as though Jesus Christ is your only audience."

Dave thought back to the year before in Amarillo, which had been the happiest time in his life. He finally knew for whom he was living. He knew his audience. And seeing Jesus as his only audience had taken the pressure off himself. He did his best to bring glory to God, not himself. If he lost, the loss hurt of course, but it wouldn't change anything truly important because God loved him and would always be with him.

Dave left for the game that night feeling better than anytime since he'd been "called up." He pitched an inning, giving up one run, but he did okay. And when he saw Jan after the game, he grinned and told her, "The feeling is back."

He went on to pitch in thirty-one games for the Padres that season—mostly in relief. He finished with a 5–3 record and a very impressive ERA of only 2.57. In 1983 Dave started twenty-eight games for the Padres and compiled a record of 14–10 in his first full season in the majors. The following year Dave started and relieved for a San Diego team that went all the way to the World Series. Dave pitched in relief five times during post-season play and never gave up an earned run.

In '85 Dave started again for the Padres and went 13–11 for the year. He only tallied nine wins against eleven losses the following year, but his ERA remained a very respectable 3.07.

Almost halfway through the '87 season, Dave got word that he'd been traded to the San Francisco Giants. As hard as it was to leave his friends on the Padres and to suddenly pick up and relocate Jan, Tiffany, and their baby son, Jonathan, to a new city where they knew hardly anyone, it looked like a good career move.

It was late in that season when he first noticed the lump—a firm, round shape about the size of a quarter under the skin on his left arm. He showed it to the trainer, who didn't think it anything to worry about. And since it didn't hurt, Dave paid it no attention. He had other things to think about— like winning seven games as a starter for a Giants team that captured their division and faced the St. Louis Cardinals in the playoffs. The Cards won the first game 5–3. Dave started in game two of the series in St. Louis, a must-win situation.

The night was cold, with a black October sky overhead. The crowd was loud. Dave remembers, "I wasn't nervous. Excited, yet totally absorbed in the game. I saw my catcher. I saw his glove. I didn't see much else. I was in the groove."

When San Francisco jumped out to a 2–0 lead in the top of the second inning, Busch Stadium fell absolutely quiet. And Dave kept them quiet by pitching the game of his life. Every time the crowd stirred, Dave silenced them again. "It was an incredible feeling of power," he says. "I was locked in. Fifty thousand fans didn't exist for me. Even the batters barely existed. Only my catcher was there. He knew what I wanted to throw. I knew that he knew. Some of the time we didn't even use signs."

Inning after inning Dave mowed down the Cards. In the fourth the Giants scored again to make it 3–0. In the eighth they got two more, and Dave coasted home with his first post-season victory. He'd given up only two hits, no runs, and had put himself in the record books. Adding to his 1984 playoff totals, he'd run his post-season scoreless streak to nineteen and two-thirds innings.

After the game he was summoned to the interview room. It was so jammed he could hardly make his way to the microphone. Someone was asking Giants' manager Roger Craig about Christian ballplayers maybe being too nice to be winners. Roger said, "They say Christians don't have any guts? Well, this guy's a Christian, and he's not afraid of anything!" And he handed the microphone to Dave.

"How do you respond to that?" a reporter asked.

It seemed to Dave that they were asking whether or not Christians are wimps. So he thought the best way to answer the question was to ask, since Christians are followers of Christ, if Jesus was a wimp? Dave told them he believed that if Jesus were in his shoes and called to compete as a professional athlete, he would play with more intensity and aggressiveness than any other athlete—but he would always be in control. He also told the reporters, "Jesus Christ is my example. I play for him. When I play, I play to glorify God. I recognize the ability he's given me, and so I play with everything I have."

Dave loved getting a chance to talk about his faith in the public eye. When Jan met him coming out of the clubhouse, he excitedly told her all about it. What a night! He'd pitched a shutout in the playoffs and then had a chance to witness for God to reporters and people from all over the country. To top it all off, that day was the Draveckys' ninth anniversary.

Jan grinned at Dave's excitement and told him, "I don't know how you're ever going to top this."

Dave started again in the sixth game of the series with the Giants leading three games to two. He pitched almost as well as he did in game two, but this time the Cardinals won the game 1–0 on a sacrifice fly in the second inning. The next night Dave's buddy Atlee Hammacker got hit hard and the Giants went home to watch the rest of playoffs and the World Series on television.

As painful as it was to lose in the playoffs, Dave spent the winter knowing he'd pitched the best baseball of his life in the most important games of his life. He could hardly wait for the next season. During the off-season Dave got the lump on his arm checked. Doctors did an MRI (Magnetic Resonance Imaging) test. The results indicated no need for concern, and the doctors told him to have it checked again in six months.

When Roger Craig named Dave as his opening day starter, and he won the first game of the season for the Giants on a three-hitter, he came home and told Jan, "You know something, baby? I think 1988 is going to be my year!"

But it wouldn't work out that way.

The '88 season turned out to be a wild roller-coaster ride for Dave. One moment he was on top pitching great, the next he was hurtling down and wondering if anything could ever stop the fall. The downturn began early in the season when his shoulder started hurting. In May he went on the disabled list. When rest didn't help, he finally had shoulder surgery.

While he was recuperating from that, his friend Atlee bugged him about getting the lump looked at again. "It's getting bigger," he said. Despite his friend's urging, Dave was more worried about his shoulder. The surgery hadn't done anything to relieve the pain. He still couldn't pitch and the team wasn't doing well, so as the season neared its end, Dave asked the Giants' permission to return home to Ohio. They said fine.

Dave couldn't deny that the lump on his arm was growing—big as a golf ball and hard like one, too—so he went for another MRI just before he left San Francisco. A few days later the doctor called him in Ohio and told him he needed to follow up with a doctor near his home. So Dave and Jan drove to Cleveland for the appointment.

They sat in a small examining room, talking quietly together, when they heard people shuffling around outside the door. Apparently Dr. Bergfield had arrived. They knew the doctor was looking at Dave's MRI because they heard the film slapped into position over the lights. Then Jan and Dave heard a deep voice speaking four distinct words: "Look at that tumor."

6

TUMOR?

Tumor? Someone had said "tumor." Everyone from friends and trainers to doctors had called this thing in Dave's arm a "lump." The lab report from the first MRI had called it a "hematoma." Jan and Dave had talked about the possibility of "scar tissue." But that was the first time anyone had used the word *tumor*.

That one word made a big difference. Tumors can be benign or malignant. If this tumor were malignant, that would mean that Dave had cancer. Suddenly, the lump that neither of them had really worried about was pretty scary. Dave and Jan looked at each other.

"I think we'd better pray," Jan whispered.

"Yeah," David responded. "We better pray right now."

And they did. David got off the examination table and sat in a chair beside his wife. They held hands and prayed.

"Dear God, we don't know what's happening. We don't know what this means. Help us to get through it, no matter what is involved. Help us to face whatever comes."

Moments later, Dr. John Bergfield walked into the room. He took Dave's arm and examined it, moving it this way and that. Then he said, "Dave, this may be a tumor. We need to do a biopsy. I'm going to send you up to see an oncologist."

That word *oncologist* scared Jan and Dave even more. They both knew that an oncologist is a doctor who specializes in cancer.

Dr. Bergfield helped them feel better when he said, "I don't think this is a malignant tumor. You've had it for over a year now, and the rate of growth is much slower than we would normally expect for a malignancy. But we need to be sure."

Before Dave could see the oncologist, they took even more X rays of the tumor. Then Dave and Jan went to the fifth floor of the hospital and met Dr. Muschler.

He examined Dave's arm again, moving it up and down and pushing on the lump. Then he repeated what Dr. Bergfield had said. "I don't think we're dealing with a malignant tumor. But we can't be sure." He thought it was probably a benign, fibrous tumor, not cancer.

When David asked when they ought to have a biopsy done, Dr. Muschler answered, "As soon as possible."

On the drive home from the hospital, neither Dave nor Jan had much to say to each other. They were in shock, both feeling as if their world had turned upside down. Every now and then, Jan would start to say something, but then she would stop. Neither she nor Dave knew what to think or what to say.

Two days later, Dave went in to the hospital for the biopsy. The doctors numbed Dave's arm. Then they made a small incision and through that cut they pulled out a small piece of the tumor. After the biopsy was finished, Dr. Muschler came into the recovery room to talk to the Draveckys. He told them the tumor was growing on the base of the deltoid muscle. And he drew a picture to help them see that the deltoid muscle is the large, shield-shaped muscle that wraps over the top of the shoulder.

And he repeated what they had heard over and over, that he didn't think the tumor was malignant.

"But I can't be one hundred percent sure," he cautioned.

Before Jan and Dave left the hospital, one of Dr. Muschler's assistants gave Dave a card with his phone number on it and said, "I used to play professional football. When I left that, it was really difficult for me. If you need to talk to somebody over the next few months, give me a call and we can get together. Maybe I can help."

Neither Dave nor Jan knew what to think about his offer. Only later did they realize that this man, like all of the doctors, were assuming that the tumor—even if it was benign—meant the end of Dave's baseball career.

Dave was discouraged. On the way home all he could think about was the fact that there was a tumor in his body—something that wasn't supposed to be a part of him—and it was growing. Taking a more optimistic approach, Jan was encouraged by what the doctor had said. After all, the doctors didn't think the lump would be malignant.

For the next two days, while he waited for the results from the biopsy, David played ball with his children. He walked into their bedrooms at night and watched them sleep. He thought about how much he loved them. He watched Jan and thought about how much he loved her. He did not want to die and leave them. Yet he knew that if the tumor in his arm did take his life, he would be in heaven with Jesus. That thought helped him feel a little better as he waited for the two days that seemed to last a lifetime.

They were still waiting for the results of the biopsy when Jan's cousin Mark called. Mark was a cancer surgeon in Texas, and he wanted to know if Dave and Jan had heard anything from Dr. Muschler. When Jan told him they hadn't heard back, he offered to call and find out the results. When he called them about an hour later, Jan answered the phone.

Dave stood in the living room and listened to Jan's end of the conversation.

The preliminary results, Mark told them, showed cancer.

Mark said quickly, "But if Dave had to get cancer, this is the kind you would want it to be."

Mark explained that it was a desmoid tumor, a kind of cancer that is slow growing and not likely to spread to other parts of the body. So this tumor—even though it was cancer—was not likely to cause Dave's death. It would, however, do a lot of damage to his arm. Dave could expect it to continue to grow and spread. The only treatment for this kind of cancer was surgery, and the doctors needed to cut every last bit of the cancer out of Dave's arm or it could come back.

Mark told them, "Dave needs to get it out of his body right away. It can do nothing but harm."

One week later Dave, Jan, and Dave's mother drove to see Dr. Muschler for the final biopsy report. Dave drove along, happy to be alive. He was glad to finally know what was going on with the lump in his arm.

Jan was worried—about the tumor and the cancer, of course, but also about whether or not the Giants would want Dave to postpone the surgery and try to pitch for one more season.

Dr. Muschler told them many of the same things they had learned from Mark. The best treatment for a desmoid tumor was surgery, and they would need to take out a large margin around the tumor, just to be sure they were getting all the cancer cells.

The problem, Dr. Muschler explained, was that the tumor was resting on the humerus bone. Ordinarily they would take out a large section of the bone. But Dr. Muschler wanted to try something else—a new treatment called cryosurgery that he thought would work better. He could cut right to the edge of the bone, then use liquid nitrogen to freeze the portion of tumor near the bone. The nitrogen would kill all the cells, both the cancer cells and the living bone cells, but it would be less damaging to Dave's arm.

Dave, Jan, and Dave's mom all asked questions—about the procedure, about what else could be done. Then Dave asked the million-dollar question: "What about my career?"

"Dave," Dr. Muschler replied quietly, "if you have this operation, I think your chances of returning to professional baseball are zero."

Dave assumed, at first, that by professional baseball Dr. Muschler meant the major leagues.

"That's okay," Dave said, "I don't mind pitching minor-league ball and working my way back up."

"Dave, I don't think you understood me," Dr. Muschler interrupted. "Losing half your deltoid muscle will take away one of the three most powerful muscles in your arm. I hope that after intensive therapy you will be able to play catch with your son in your backyard."

Everyone in that room got quiet.

Finally, Dave said, "No professional ball at all?"

"No," Dr. Muschler answered.

Dave immediately replied, "Hey, Doc, if that's the way it is, let's get on with it. I've had a great career. I've been in an All Star game, pitched in two National League championships, and played in one World Series. And coaches told me I'd never throw a pitch in the major leagues! I've enjoyed every minute of it, and I'm ready to go on with whatever is next.

"If I never play again, I'll know that God has someplace else he wants me. I also believe in a

God who does miracles. If God wants me to pitch, I'll pitch, with or without a deltoid muscle."

Then they set the date for the surgery: October 6. That was Jan and Dave's wedding anniversary. Exactly one year earlier, Dave had pitched a winning game in the National League championship.

That night, Dave and Jan told their children about the tumor—and the surgery—and that their daddy would probably never be able to play baseball again.

Tiffany thought for a moment and then asked, "We won't have to move anymore? I can stay in the same school, and we can live near Grandma and Grandpa all the time?"

Jonathan suddenly understood. "Dad," he said, "you mean you'll be able to play football with me every day?"

When Jan and Dave nodded yes, both children began to cheer.

7

THE OPERATION

The day before the operation, Dave and Jan asked their pastor to do something they had read about in the Bible. James 5:14 says that when someone is sick, the elders of their church should come together and pray for them. So the night before Dave went into the hospital for surgery, about twenty-five members of the Tabernacle Evangelical Presbyterian Church met in a room near the sanctuary to pray for Dave and Jan.

Dave sat in a chair in the middle of the group. Pastor Bob Stauffer put his hand on Dave's shoulder where the surgeons would be cutting. Others, who were close enough, rested their hands on Dave. One by one people began to pray.

They asked God to keep Dave in his hands. They prayed for the surgeons and asked God to give Dave and Jan a feeling of peace, no matter what the result of the operation would be. As Dave sat there, he was filled with peace and a sense of being enveloped by God's love and care.

After most of the others had left, Reverend Stauffer spoke to Dave alone. He said, "While we were praying for you, the weirdest thing happened. My hand got really hot—so hot I had to take it off your arm. I don't know what that means, but I am sure that God is at work tonight."

Dave left the prayer meeting convinced that he was in the hands of a loving God.

The next morning Dave, Jan, and Dave's mom drove up to Cleveland. Dave spent the day having tests and having his blood drawn. At 5:30 A.M. the following day he checked into the hospital. Before the operation began, Dave told the doctors and nurses, "I want you to know something. A lot of people are praying for you right now. God is in control, and I have all the confidence in the world in each one of you."

Once Dave was under the anesthesia, Dr. Muschler began to cut out the tumor, slowly and carefully, keeping a margin of healthy flesh on every side of the tumor. He was careful to protect the radial nerve; if that were damaged, Dave would lose the use of his hand. He gently separated the other muscles from the deltoid muscle. Finally, in order to get all the tumor, he cut out over half of the deltoid muscle.

Then all that was left was separating the tumor from the humerus bone. That was where Dr. Muschler used the cryosurgery: cutting a little, then freezing the tissue. Each small section of bone and tumor had to be frozen, then thawed, then frozen again three times before he could pry the tumor up and move on to the next small section. Dr. Muschler went through that process ten times before he was able to lift all the tumor out of Dave's arm.

Meanwhile, Jan and Dave's mom were in the waiting room. When Dave had been taken into surgery before 7 A.M., Dr. Muschler had told them that the operation would take about four hours. So Jan thought that Dave would be out before noon.

Instead, they watched as the other people in the waiting room were called and told that their loved one was out of surgery and in recovery. No one called for them.

Finally, at about 1:30 P.M., Dr. Bergfield phoned from the operating room to tell them that the surgery was taking longer than expected, but that things were going well. He cautioned Jan that Dave would be "handicapped," but that she shouldn't worry.

Jan was disappointed. She had been hoping secretly that the doctors would cut Dave's arm open and find that God had miraculously healed the tumor. That it would be gone—or have mysteriously turned into nothing more serious than scar tissue. Dr. Bergfield's phone call crushed that hope, and Jan didn't understand what he meant by Dave being "handicapped." That worried her too.

Jan continued praying. Hour after hour passed. Finally, at 5:30 P.M., a nurse told Jan that Dave was in recovery and the doctor would be out to talk with her in a few minutes. But he didn't come out until after 6 P.M., and then to tell Jan that a problem had developed: lying on his side for such a long surgery had reduced the blood circulation in Dave's leg. They were taking him back to surgery for an emergency procedure to restore circulation and to relieve pain in his leg. This second surgery took another long, exhausting two hours.

Dr. Muschler finally came back into the waiting room to sit down and tell Jan all about the surgery. He had taken more than half of Dave's deltoid muscle, and his leg was finally okay. He told her that, with extensive therapy, one day Dave might be able to lift his arm over his head— but he probably never would be able to reach into his back pocket and take out his wallet.

Jan looked at Dr. Muschler and said, "In other words, short of a miracle, he will never pitch again."

Dr. Muschler looked Jan straight in the eye and answered, "Yes, short of a miracle, he will never pitch again."

Dave stayed in the hospital five more days. He was in a lot of pain, not only from his arm, but from his leg.

Finally, the day came for him to go home. As soon as he got into the car, he turned to Jan and said, "Take me to Arby's!"

After Dave had eaten one hot ham and cheese sandwich, one turkey deluxe, and a large order of curly fries, he felt better. As they continued home, he knew that he still had a long way to go just to get well.

The following Thursday night, Dave watched the Dodgers and the A's play in the final game of the World Series. The game wasn't even close, and Jan went on to bed early. Dave stayed up to see the end of the game. When Orel Hershiser made the last pitch and the other Dodgers ran out onto the field to celebrate, Dave thought about his last baseball season. He had pitched so well in that first game of the season against these same Dodgers! He had thought that this year would be his year. Instead, his baseball career was over. Dave sat in the darkness and cried.

Dave and Jan had been building a house in Boardman, Ohio, the small town where they had grown up. The house wasn't finished yet, so while

Dave recuperated, they lived in the basement of his parents' home. Most days, Dave went over to their building site and checked on what the construction workers were doing. The work seemed to be going very slowly.

And, on a sofa bed in his parent's basement, neither Jan nor Dave were getting much sleep. Dave was in a lot of pain from both his arm and his leg, and he was suffering from bad headaches. At the end of his first week out of the hospital, Dave and Jan went to church. That morning, the pastor asked if anyone had something they wanted to share—either a prayer request or something they were thankful for.

Dave stood up, leaning on his cane, and spoke. "I want to thank you all for your prayers. During the week I was in the hospital, I had a tremendous sense of peace. Your prayers made a difference." Then he paused and said, "I've come to the place where if I never play baseball again, it's okay with me." Dave and Jan cried, right there in the middle of church.

Two weeks after the surgery, Dave went back to Dr. Muschler to have his stitches checked. When the doctor asked him to try to raise his arm over his head—a movement they had expected to take months to accomplish—Dave slowly lifted his arm over his head.

"That is amazing!" Dr. Muschler told him.

Each day in therapy Dave worked hard to retrain other muscles to take over the work originally done by the missing deltoid muscle. Only five weeks after the surgery, Dave came home from therapy and said to Jan, "Hey, watch this!"

Using his left arm, he reached into his back pocket, pulled out his wallet, and placed it on the counter.

"Wow!" Jan exclaimed. That was the motion that the doctors had said would take months of therapy, and that Dave might never be able to do again.

"That's not all," Dave told her. He stood for a moment, pretending to hold a baseball in his left hand. Then, slowly, he went through his pitching motion.

Jan began to cry. "I can't believe it," she sobbed. She and Dave began to hope that, one day, he would be able to pitch again.

Dave's therapy was hard work. It started with Ken Johnson, his physical therapist, moving Dave's arm, because Dave couldn't move it himself. Then, when Dave could do the exercises himself, they added a one-pound weight, attached with Velcro to his wrist. Dave moved that little one-pound weight around for an hour—and at first that hour of exercise left him exhausted! Slowly, he worked his way up to two pounds, then three, then all the way up to five-pound weights on his wrist. Dave didn't know if he would ever pitch again, but he did know that he had to work, and work hard, to do what he could to regain the use of his arm. God would have to do the rest.

On November 18, six weeks after the surgery, Dave and Jan finally moved into their new home. Coupled with the progress Dave was making in physical therapy, it seemed like a promising new beginning. They celebrated Christmas in their new house.

On January 9, three months after Dave's operation, he had a checkup at the Cleveland Clinic. Dave was excited, anticipating the surprise he would give the doctors when they saw what he could do with his arm.

Dr. Bergfield and his associates came in first to examine him. Indeed, they were amazed at Dave's progress. When they left, Dr. Muschler came in and said to Dave, "Show me what you can do."

Dave started with the movements that he knew the doctor would expect. Then he went on to motions he knew would astonish him. He started with his hand by his side and pushed it straight back. Dave could now push his left arm back, just as far as his right. Then he lifted his arm straight out from his body. Dr. Muschler could hardly believe what he was seeing. He got up, walked over to Dave, and put his hands on Dave's shoulder.

"Do that again!" He felt the muscles moving in Dave's arm, trying to figure out what was enabling Dave's arm to move in that way.

"You must be using your lats!" he commented.

Dr. Bergfield and his associates came back into the room, and all five doctors watched Dave perform his movements.

Bergfield turned to Muschler and said, "You see? I told you that you weren't dealing with an ordinary individual here. He's an athlete, and they are different!"

"I am really impressed!" Dr. Muschler responded.

"Well," said Bergfield, "let's get him throwing. What do you think, George? Can he throw?"

Muschler was cautious, however. X rays indicated that the bone was healing itself nicely, but the parts of the bone that had been frozen would break more easily than normal for at least one year following the surgery. Plus, cryosurgery was too new; no one knew how long it would take the bone to get strong again. Certainly, no one whose bone had been frozen had ever tried to pitch a baseball at ninety miles an hour. What's more, no one had ever tried to pitch professional baseball without a deltoid muscle in his pitching arm.

8

ON TOP OF THE WORLD

Dave was so anxious to start playing baseball that he made the last two days of spring training in March, just so he could put on his spikes and walk onto a baseball diamond. He played a little catch with Atlee and did a bit of running in the Arizona sun. Everyone who saw him throw was amazed. Dave felt great. He told everyone who would listen that he was coming back and would pitch before the summer was over.

Back in San Francisco in April, the Giants' physical therapist, Larry Brown, put him through some arm exercises and then suggested they go out and throw. After three pitches he stopped Dave and asked, "How are you doing that?" It wasn't that Dave was throwing even near to normal speed, but his arm motion was the same as it had been pre-surgery. Since he was missing most of a major arm muscle, the therapist had assumed Dave's delivery would be drastically different.

Dave walked over to him, his glove under his arm, and told him, "Larry, I think you should understand where I'm coming from. As far as I'm concerned, this has all been a miracle of God."

With a puzzled look on his face, Larry said, "There's no other way to explain it."

Yet, after a few weeks of therapy and throwing, Dave began to get discouraged. No matter what he did, he couldn't seem to throw the ball any harder. He felt as if his arm was dead. To make matters worse, his shoulder began to hurt. He took a couple days off and tried again. His shoulder felt as if someone had hammered a nail into it. So the doctor and the therapist decided he should quit all his workouts—no exercise, no throwing—for a whole month.

"Teammates were feeling sorry for me," Dave admits, "and I was feeling sorry for myself." He showed up at practice and wore a uniform to games. But he says, "I didn't feel like a real base-ball player. I felt more like a ghost."

The first time he threw after his month of rest, Dave felt a little soreness, so he took a day off and threw some more. Unfortunately, the pain became unbearable. He went home so discouraged he told Jan, "I don't think I'm gonna be able to do it."

The following day he told Atlee his arm hurt and he couldn't throw, but Atlee suggested they play some catch. "I'd better not," Dave told him.

"What have you got to lose?" Atlee asked. "You've done your therapy. Your arm is strong. Don't baby it. The time has come. Let it rip."

So they started throwing the ball back and forth. The longer Dave threw, the better his shoulder felt. When he admitted he was feeling pretty good, Atlee told him, "All right. Let's throw through some of that pain. Let's air this baby out!" He backed up and they began to throw hard. Amazingly, Dave's arm began to feel as if it had a little life in it. Within a few days, Dave was throwing from the mound. A couple days after that, pitching coach Norm Sherry suggested Dave throw some batting practice. He was definitely making progress again.

Dave had another MRI done on July 6. The doctor noticed that a lump seemed to have filled in the gap where the muscle had been removed. He said it might be the tumor again; it was too soon to tell. Dave didn't worry about it because the coaches had scheduled a simulated game pitching against some of his own teammates under game conditions. He threw three innings— about sixty pitches—and showed pretty good control. His fastball reached about eighty-two miles an hour; at his best Dave had reached about eighty-eight.

A few days later, Dave pitched a five-inning simulated game. A hundred pitches. The arm felt fine, he had better control, and he got most of the batters out. Then Norm Sherry told him to really air out the last five or six pitches to see what he could do. Dave's arm still felt great as he jogged over to the screen and asked, "How fast was I?"

"You got up to eighty-five."

"Fantastic!" Dave exclaimed. Only three miles per hour less than his best. "I'm fired up now."

He turned to Norm Sherry. "Hey, Norm! I'm ready for some real competition. I want to go down to Phoenix and get some guys out. What do you think?"

Dave hoped to do his rehab with San Francisco's triple-A farm club in Phoenix. Instead, the Giants assigned him to the San Jose Giants to test him in single-A-level ball—the lowest rung on the minor-league ladder.

San Jose was playing a series in nearby Stockton. So after the Bay area radio stations announced Dave would be pitching, the game was sold out. Fans were lining up two hours before game time. In the clubhouse Dave took time to pray. He bowed his head in front of his locker and put the whole game before God. He told the Lord that he trusted him with his life and that he wanted to glorify God—win or lose.

When Dave walked out onto the field, the fans went nuts. The stadium wasn't big, but it was bulging. People stood everywhere, pressing up against the fence, straining to see, making noise. It was a minor-league game, but Dave had major-league jitters.

After San Jose scored in the top of the first, Dave took the mound with a 1–0 lead. He toed the rubber and took a deep breath. The leadoff batter fouled off his first two pitches for strikes. Then he hit a weak fly ball to left and Dave had his first out. It felt great. Two quick outs later, Dave was back in the dugout, kidding around with the guys. People told him later they had never seen anyone have so much fun playing baseball. It wasn't an act. After all he'd been through, Dave was having fun again.

He went through the first three innings without giving up a hit. After surrendering a single in the fourth, he picked the runner off and went on to retire the side. The fifth and sixth innings went quickly. Still, he was beginning to tire by the seventh and final inning of the game. (Since it was the first of a doubleheader scheduled that day, the game was two innings shorter than usual.)

The first Stockton hitter in the bottom of the seventh smoked a double. Dave got the next guy on a fly ball before putting the tying run on base by walking the next man. The next batter popped a bunt down the third-base line. Dave took two lunging steps and dove flat out trying to catch it and double off the runners. He got his glove on the ball, but when he hit the ground the ball popped loose. He grabbed the ball, and when his catcher yelled, "Third! Third!" he threw from his knees to force the runner. Two outs.

"I don't remember how I got the last out," Dave says. "I just remember all the players gathering on the mound, slapping me and yelling as though they had won a play-off game. The crowd was yelling too.

"When I search through my baseball memories," Dave says, "I don't find any game happier than that one. I was on top of the world."

Dave thought a complete-game shutout would earn him a trip to Phoenix for his next start, but the Giants wanted him to pitch again for the San Jose Giants in Reno, Nevada. The old stadium in Reno was nearly full. Once again, people had heard about the comeback and wanted to see for themselves.

Dave gave up a three-run homer early. In the fourth, Dave says, "It was as though the floodlights suddenly switched on. It happened. I locked in. Up until then, even in Stockton, I hadn't felt it. I'd pitched all right, but this was better than 'all right.' I felt I could hit a spot with my eyes closed. My breaking ball started snapping. For the last five innings, I shut down the Reno team, completed the game, threw about a hundred pitches, and won 7–3."

In the clubhouse after the game Dave called Al Rosen, the Giants' general manager. Rosen told Dave that he could move up to Phoenix—the next step after that would be the major leagues.

Before the game with Phoenix, Dave again took time to pray. He didn't ask God for success. Rather, he prayed that the Lord would either swing the door to the majors wide open, or slam it shut. He didn't want anything left unclear. Dave's drive to succeed was so strong, he thought he might push himself into a situation he wasn't ready for—either physically or spiritually.

By the way the game went, there was no doubt which way the door was swinging. Dave pitched his best yet. He threw seven scoreless innings without walking a soul. He was locked in again. It was that old familiar feeling. In the eighth he gave up two runs that cut the lead to one. Yet when the manager asked if he wanted to go back out for the ninth, Dave didn't hesitate. "This baby's mine," he said. He wanted to win or lose it himself.

He shut down the opposition in the final inning and won the game 3–2. He'd given up seven hits, struck out three, and walked none. After the game Dave made a beeline for the clubhouse looking for Bob Kennedy, a Giants official who'd flown down from San Francisco just to watch him pitch.

"Mr. Kennedy! Mr. Kennedy! Did you talk to Al Rosen yet?" Dave wanted to know.

When he learned Kennedy had just hung up, Dave asked him, "What did he say? Don't you think I'm ready for the big leagues?"

"If you get a little more work, maybe a few more games . . ."

Dave knew he was playing with him, so he dropped to his knees and pretended to beg, "Please. I'm ready. Please send me to San Francisco."

Bob Kennedy looked down and finally smiled. "Pack your bags," he told Dave. "You're going back to the big leagues."

9

THE COMEBACK MIRACLE

When he got back to San Francisco, Jan kept saying, "David, I just can't believe this."

"To us," Dave says, "my return to the majors was a miracle. But it was *our* miracle." The Draveckys still didn't realize just how many other people were excited about *their* miracle—until Tuesday, when Roger Craig named Dave as his starter against the Reds on Thursday.

Dave's parents had flown in so they could see him pitch. It was his dad who mentioned something he'd heard on the radio. "David," he asked, "do you know anything about this Alex Vlahos thing on KNBR?"

"I don't think so," Dave said. Alex was a little boy who had leukemia. Dave had visited this boy a couple months before at Stanford Children's Hospital.

"Then you better listen to this," Dave's dad said as he turned on the radio to the station that broadcasts Giants games. Within a minute they heard a request for listeners to make a pledge for every pitch Dave would throw in Thursday's game. The money would go to the Life-Savers Foundation to test possible donors for bone marrow transplants of the kind Alex needed.

Any hope of successful treatment for Alex Vlahos would depend on finding a donor who was a perfect match. For two people who were unrelated, the odds were one in fifteen thousand, so a lot of potential donors needed to be tested. Alex's parents figured if Dave would visit their son, local TV and radio stations would cover the visit and publicize the appeal for a donor. So when one of the Giants' front office employees came to Dave with the idea of the hospital visit, he agreed in a heartbeat.

Dave and Alex met on the front lawn of the hospital. Alex was all boy, a six-year-old bundle of energy who wasn't a bit awed by the cameras and microphones crowded around him. He told Dave he was a big Giants fan and his favorite players were Will Clark and Kevin Mitchell.

They played catch for a while and Dave tossed Alex some pitches he could hit with a plastic bat. At one point when a reporter was asking Dave about his faith, Alex looked up and said, "You love God a lot, don't you, Dave?"

"I sure do, Alex," Dave told him.

"I do too," Alex said. "I love Jesus."

After their meeting, Dave sent Alex some small Giants souvenirs. He tried to stay in touch with Alex and his parents, who appreciated the attention Dave had helped generate for their son. But what had happened back in June was nothing like the publicity now. Every radio and television station in San Francisco carried the story. By game time, the money pledged for Alex was more than a thousand dollars a pitch. The news was all "Dave Dravecky and little Alex Vlahos."

Dave thought he was too excited to sleep Wednesday night, but he zonked out and slept so long that Jan had to wake him up to go to the ballpark the next morning. Before he left, the family prayed. Jan and Dave sat on the edge of their bed with Tiffany and Jonathan standing next to them. They held hands and said some very simple words.

They had no idea how the game might go. Even when Dave had all the muscles in his arm, he never knew for sure if he'd be able to pitch a great game, or if he'd get clobbered. So they prayed for peace and calm, no matter what happened on the field. They didn't pray to win; they never did that. They prayed that Dave's performance would glorify God, that he'd have the right attitude and focus. They thanked God for bringing Dave back to this point.

As they prayed, Jan began to cry. Her tears upset Jonathan who said, "What's wrong, Mommy?"

Jan was too choked up to even answer, so Dave explained that she wasn't sad. "Those are tears of joy because Daddy is going to pitch again."

Before the game Dave went to his manager Roger Craig and told him he had two requests. He'd like Terry Kennedy to catch the game because he'd been a teammate in San Diego and had caught Dave's very first big-league game. Roger agreed. Then came request number two. Dave admitted to his manager he didn't know how he would pitch, but no matter how well or how poorly he did, could Roger please let him go at least a hundred pitches—for Alex Vlahos.

Roger laughed and told Dave he appreciated the sentiment and he hoped Dave could throw a complete game. He'd let him go as long as he could, but the Giants needed to win this one. Just before game time, several players and one of the coaches walked over to Dave's locker and said they'd like to pray with him. After praying, Dave finished putting on his Giants uniform with number 43 across the back.

Fifteen minutes before the game Dave walked down the runway from the clubhouse and onto the field to face a sea of lenses all pointed at him. As the cameras clicked and whirred, Dave turned to his pitching coach and said, "Holy smokes, Norm! What's going on?"

By the time Dave hurried to the bullpen to begin warming up, 34,810 fans were on their feet screaming, cheering, and giving him a standing ovation. The reception seemed so incredible that Dave looked at his catcher, grabbed a bit of the jersey over his heart, and pounded it up and down to show him how his pulse was hammering. Terry Kennedy grinned back and signaled that his heart was doing the same thing.

As Dave warmed up, he began to calm down. When he was ready to walk to the dugout, the fans rose again—cheering wildly and calling things like "Go get 'em, Dave," and "Glad you're back, Dave."

Moments later, when Dave jogged out to take the mound, the center field scoreboard flashed a gigantic, "Welcome back, Dave!" and the crowd roared and rose to its feet once again. Dave stood holding the ball, rubbing it, looking at Terry Kennedy. As he jerked off his cap and waved it to acknowledge the cheers, the emotion of it all overcame Dave. After ten months of struggle and uncertainty—now this. Looking around and up at the rows and rows of cheering people, Dave says, "I had no words to describe my emotion. My heart was so full."

He stepped off the mound to gather himself, and he thought, *Now is the time to say thank you, Lord. Thank you for the privilege of doing this again. Thank you that you restored my arm so I could pitch. But most of all, thank you for what you've done for me ... for saving me ... and for your love in Jesus Christ.*

That prayer took only a few moments. Then Dave stepped back up on the mound and started throwing. From the first pitch, he was locked in. His rhythm and balance were perfect. Terry Kennedy was reading his mind. Dave was in that groove where he and Terry may as well have been playing catch in that backyard in Boardman, Ohio, because it seemed like no one else was around.

Of course the Cincinnati Reds were around; they'd come to play. When a sports writer asked Pete Rose, the Reds' manager, if he'd thought about the difficulty of what Dave was trying to do, Pete spit out a sunflower seed. "No," he said bluntly. "He's back, and that's great for him. I hope he loses."

Dave got the first hitter to pop out on a short fly to center. One out. The cheers rained down again. The second batter hit the second pitch and grounded out to third. When the next batter, Eric Davis, one of the toughest hitters in baseball, also grounded out to third and Dave ran for the dugout, the entire crowd stood to cheer again.

That's how it went for seven innings. Every time Dave finished off the Reds and trotted in from the mound, the crowd stood and cheered. Roger Craig said later that in all the decades he'd played and coached, he'd never seen so much emotion at a game. Jan, watching from the stands, cried continuously for two hours.

Despite all that was happening around him, and the fact that he hadn't pitched a major-league game in over a year, Dave had near-perfect control. Only four times did he even go to three balls on a batter. He walked one and entered the eighth inning having given up just one hit. In the meantime his teammates spotted Dave a 4–0 lead.

He needed those runs in the eighth when a bloop single, a double, and a two-out, three-run homer suddenly cut the lead to one. It all happened so quickly there wasn't time to warm up a reliever before Dave got the final out and walked to the dugout for yet another standing ovation.

Dave knew he was done. Sure enough, the manager pinch hit for him in the bottom of the eighth and called Steve Bedrosian, the Giants' stopper, to finish off the Reds in the ninth. When Bedrosian went to the mound to warm up, the crowd started yelling. It took Dave a minute to realize they were cheering for him. They wouldn't stop.

Terry Kennedy called to him over the din, "Go on out there. It's your day. Take a bow. C'mon, get going."

So Dave did. He walked out of the dugout and onto the field, looking up again at the rows upon rows of fans now screaming their lungs out. He lifted his cap. It was his twelfth standing ovation of the day. When he disappeared back into the dugout the fans still wouldn't stop. They wanted Dave again.

The other players gestured at him. "C'mon, Dave, go out again." So he walked up the steps, looked up at those thousands and thousands of people, and lifted both hands in thanks.

Bedrosian threw bullets. Cincinnati went down one, two, three.

Dave jumped to his feet before the last swinging strike, and Terry Kennedy grabbed him for a big hug. Then everyone ran out onto the field where all of his teammates took turns embracing and congratulating Dave. The fans continued to cheer, yelling as though they would never stop, until long after everyone had walked off the field.

Jan hadn't seen the last outs. The ballpark security staff had wanted to get her out of the stadium as soon as Dave finished pitching, so they led her and the kids toward the clubhouse where she waited in the tunnel the bullpen guys use to get to the locker room. When two of the relievers spotted her, they insisted she come on into the clubhouse.

In all Dave's years in baseball, Jan had never been in the locker room. The only women allowed in were reporters. Jan was embarrassed, but the guys were excited about taking her to Dave.

Jan saw Dave standing in front of his locker, still in his uniform. He saw her, and she walked toward him with her arms outstretched. "Oh, David," was all she could say. As Dave hugged her tightly he looked around the room. Everything was absolutely quiet. All the other players were standing silently at their lockers, watching Dave and his wife. Afterwards, they came over to Jan, one by one, and hugged her too.

Dave's arm was wrapped in ice, and off he went to the post-game press conference with Jan. Everybody who was anybody in the world of news, sports, and entertainment was there. Roger Craig told the press how emotional the game had been for him and how he thought its importance reached far beyond baseball, sending a message of hope to people all over the nation who face sickness or difficulty.

When Roger finished and Dave walked to the microphone, the room grew quiet. As soon as he took the first question he realized there was something he needed to say. "It's important for me to give credit where credit is due," Dave said. "I want to give praise and glory to Jesus Christ for allowing me the opportunity to come back and play again."

He went on to credit his doctors, therapists, and trainers as well, but he wanted everyone to know that his comeback was a miracle for which God deserved praise.

The press conference lasted a long time. Many questions had to do with the future. How did Dave feel? What about the rest of the season? Dave said he hoped to continue pitching, that he felt great. He also said he would have to take the future one day at a time.

"After what happened today," he said, "anything else will be icing on the cake."

10

"IT'S BROKEN!"

Finally, it seemed to the Draveckys as if everything was back to normal. For ten months they had worried and wondered if Dave would come back. After pitching that game against the Reds on Thursday, August 10, all doubt was gone.

On Monday Dave and the rest of the Giants left on a road trip. Tuesday morning in Montreal, as he and teammate Bob Knepper visited a bookstore near their hotel, Dave told Bob how thankful he felt. "You have no idea how exciting it's been to live in the middle of a miracle. Then to get the chance to give the credit to Jesus Christ of everything I've done in baseball, that's the top."

Bob agreed that giving God credit for his comeback was a wonderful thing. "But I see another miracle," he told Dave, "the miracle God began in your life eight years ago in Amarillo. It's great God's given you another chance to pitch, but that's pretty small compared to the chance he's given you to live with him forever."

Dave realized his friend was right. He felt excited and challenged by what Bob said. Dave sensed that he ought to help other people see the bigger picture of God's love. But how?

That evening, only about twenty thousand people came to the stadium. They gave Dave no standing ovation when he walked to the mound. Everything was indeed back to normal. After three innings, Dave felt confident. He'd gone all the way through the Expos lineup without giving up a hit. When he came up to bat, he even got a hit himself.

In the fifth inning he struggled a little with his control, but Roger Craig didn't even bother warming up a reliever because Dave seemed to be cruising along. In the dugout after the fifth, Dave rubbed his left arm. It felt strange. It didn't hurt exactly; it just tingled. Brett Butler, the Giants' center fielder, noticed what he was doing and asked, "Is everything all right, Dave?"

"Yeah, everything's fine," Dave told him. "I just feel a little stiffness."

Months earlier, Dr. Muschler had warned Dave that if he ever felt any pain in his arm he should quit throwing immediately or he could break the bone. But Dave had done so much since then without the slightest problem. He never thought a little tingling might be a warning sign.

The Giants rallied in the sixth, so Dave took a 3–0 lead to the mound in the bottom of the inning with the heart of the Expos order coming up to bat. He got off to a bad start by giving up a home run to the first batter. Andres Gallaraga was next. Figuring The Big Cat would be expecting an outside pitch, Dave threw one inside. The pitch nicked Gallaraga, who trotted down to first.

Robbie Thompson, his second baseman, walked over to ask if Dave was okay. "I feel great," Dave told him.

Three thousand miles away Jan Dravecky was listening to the game on the radio and suddenly feeling very nervous. When Dave hit Gallaraga, she began muttering, "Get him out of there, Roger. Take him out before he gets into trouble." But Roger Craig couldn't hear her, and Dave continued to pitch.

Dave wasn't at all happy about putting a runner on base because that meant Tim Raines walked to the plate, representing the tying run. He was always a tough hitter. Dave would have to bear down to get him out.

Coming to his set position, Dave stared over at Gallaraga on first. Then he lifted his right leg and at the same moment brought his left hand up and back. Pushing off the rubber and striding toward the plate, Dave threw. Next to his ear he heard a loud popping noise. The crack could be heard all over the field. It sounded as though someone had snapped a heavy tree branch.

"I felt as if my arm had broken off my body and was sailing toward home plate," Dave remembers. "I grabbed at my arm, trying to catch it and pull it back." He never saw the ball leave his hand and fly high past an astonished Terry Kennedy, who went charging after it. He never thought about Gallaraga, who headed hesitantly toward second, as though he was truly guilty of stealing.

As Dave grasped his arm to keep it from flying away, he tumbled headfirst down the mound and screamed with all the air in his lungs. He did a complete 360, flopping onto the infield grass until he came to rest on his back with his feet pointing toward center field. He had never felt such pain.

Dave was writhing and groaning and still trying to get his breath when he looked up and saw his first baseman, Will Clark, standing over him. "Oh, Will, it's killing me!" he exclaimed. "It's broken! It feels like I broke my arm!"

Above and around the field, the entire stadium fell silent. As the pain gradually lessened,

Dave lay still and looked up at the circle of faces standing over him. Roger Craig leaned down and gently hugged him.

Dave remembers being amazed at what was going on. "I'd thought the book had been written on my comeback, and everything was back to normal. Now this! I wasn't, not even for a split second, angry. I was simply astonished—and somehow full of the certainty that God was writing another chapter in my life that something more, something amazing, was being revealed."

When they brought out a stretcher, Dave gritted his teeth and announced that he wanted to walk off the field. Somebody told him to shut up and lie down. He did and was quickly wheeled through a tunnel under the stands and into the training room. There in the clubhouse a doctor wrapped Dave's arm tight to his body as a handful of teammates and coaches watched. Ballplayers are not big on showing emotion, especially tender ones, but that day, emotion filled the air in the clubhouse.

After the game, Roger Craig would break into tears in front of reporters, who had to wait in embarrassed silence for a solid minute before he could begin to answer their questions. The game continued, and no sooner had Dave been carried into the clubhouse than the Expos catcher, Mike Fitzgerald, came running into the training room with all his catcher's gear on.

"Mike looked at me with tears in his eyes, grabbed me by the back of the head, and pulled me next to him," Dave recalls. "Then he hugged me and kissed me. 'I love you, brother,' he said, and then he turned and went running back out to the field. I watched him go in amazement thinking, *I'm fairly sure that's never happened in baseball before.*"

An ambulance arrived and paramedics were about to wheel Dave away when his buddy Bob Knepper put his head near Dave's and suggested they pray. Dave says he doesn't remember Bob's words. "It wasn't so much *what* he said as it was *how* he said it. Bob had a hard time getting his words out. His voice was cracking. Love for me filled his prayer."

While Bob Knepper prayed, the bottom of the sixth inning ended and the Giants players who'd been out in the field came racing into the clubhouse to check on Dave. As they entered the training room they fell silent until, by the time Bob finished his prayer, there were twenty-five guys crowded around. Dave looked up and saw that many of his teammates had tears in their eyes.

Dave says that Bob's prayer took away any remaining anxiety he felt. He knew he was in God's hands. As he was being wheeled out of the room, Dave turned to his teammates and told them, "Hey, if there was ever anything to the saying, 'Win one for me,' this is it, guys! I don't want that lead to disappear. I'm probably not going to pitch any more this season, and I want my record to be 2–0. I want to end the year undefeated."

Terry Kennedy looked as if he thought Dave had lost his mind. Then Dave greeted the ambulance driver by saying, "This has been kind of a rough day. Please get me there safely—I've had enough excitement."

11

BATTLING CANCER

Dave thought the media attention had reached an absolute peak after his comeback game victory against the Reds in San Francisco on August 10, but he soon learned that he was quite mistaken. On August 15, every late news program in the country led with the horrifying footage of Dave's arm snapping and him tumbling off the mound. By the next morning, every network wanted a special interview. Dozens of magazines and newspapers called. Hollywood was talking about making a movie.

With his arm broken, the focus suddenly shifted. The press had considered Dave's comeback a "miracle." What would they call this? The opposite of a miracle? If coming back from cancer had lifted people's spirits, should this dash them?

Dave says that wasn't how he viewed it. He says, "I saw my life as one long adventure in partnership with God. The real miracle of my life had begun in Amarillo, and it continued."

Dave told reporters he hoped to be able to return and pitch again. After coming back from cancer, coming back from a broken arm didn't seem like that big of a deal. Lots of people had done that. He also told people that the future hope of pitching again wasn't his basic source of optimism. His confidence was grounded in Jesus Christ. "When you've done everything you can and yet everything seems to have fallen apart," Dave said, "you need to know that God is there with you. He can overcome."

Previously, the press had told the world about Dave's physical recovery. "Now they marveled at my positive attitude as if that were a bigger miracle," Dave says. "In a way, maybe it was."

The medical report sounded like good news. Dave's break looked pretty ordinary, and the doctors said the bone had been weak and still recovering from being frozen. The strain of pitching had caused a hairline fracture; that's what had caused the tingling. When Dave continued to pitch, the fracture widened and the bone snapped. There was no reason to think the bone wouldn't heal in time for him to pitch the 1990 season.

Despite his optimism about the future, the next few weeks proved extremely difficult for Dave. Because of his arm, doctors didn't want him to sleep lying down, so he tossed and turned all night, getting more and more tired every day. He had a tough time doing anything with his right hand. Jan even had to help bathe him. Dave hated feeling dependent and helpless.

The worst thing of all was sitting on the bench and watching his teammates play the National League Championship Series without him. Just two years before he'd pitched the best games of his career in the playoffs against the Cardinals. This time he could only cheer for his teammates as they battled the Chicago Cubs. Dave says he felt like an invisible man.

By the time the Giants went into the fifth game leading the series three games to one, everyone was feeling good except Dave. He still couldn't sleep. "I ached," he says. "But it wasn't just my arm. My whole body ached to get into the game."

After the Giants broke a 1–1 tie to go up 3–1 in the bottom of the eighth, Dave walked back into the clubhouse to put a brace on his arm. He planned to celebrate with his team and wanted to avoid hurting his arm while he did it.

It looked like the Giants were headed for the World Series, but the game wasn't over yet. The Cubs drove in a run and had two on with two out when Chicago's great second baseman, Ryne Sandberg, came to the plate. Sandberg only managed a soft ground ball to Robby Thompson at second. He threw to first. Sandberg was out, and the Giants were National League Champions.

Everybody rushed out of the dugout toward the mound, jumping into a pile of celebrating players already piling on top of each other. Dave followed cautiously, careful of his arm. Suddenly, someone—Dave never knew who it was— slammed into him from behind, knocking him into the pile. An astounding pain blazed through his arm. It hurt as much as it had in Montreal.

Dave pulled his arm against his body, trying to protect it from the surging, leaping pile of bodies around him. Then Dusty Baker, the Giants hitting coach, and the team trainer, Mart Letendre, saw him. They pulled Dave out of the pile and led him off the field while the celebration continued.

It was another break, and the arm hurt more this time than it did the first. He not only couldn't sleep or bathe himself, he couldn't cut his own meat or even put on a coat by himself. He absolutely hated asking for help.

The World Series began five days later, and San Francisco lost the first two games in Oakland. The scores weren't even close, so the Giants came home to Candlestick Park, knowing they had a very big mountain to climb.

A few minutes before game time, Dave was sitting in front of his locker, talking to Bob Knepper, when they felt a low rumble in the floor. "That feels like an earthquake," Bob said.

"It *is* an earthquake," Dave told him

As the stadium began to shake, players ran out the door of the clubhouse toward the parking lot. By the time they reached an open area outside the stadium, the shaking had stopped. It didn't seem like that big of a deal until reporters began saying that part of the Bay Bridge had collapsed and buildings had come down in San Francisco.

The game was canceled. Since friends and relatives staying in nearby hotels didn't have electricity, Jan and Dave invited a small crowd to spend the night in their condominium. Listening to the news of their neighbors around the Bay, hearing about all the people who had died, the Draveckys felt thankful for their lives. Nevertheless, Jan and Dave went to bed that night wondering what more could happen.

They didn't have to wait long to find out.

A week later the entire Dravecky family left for home in Ohio. Dave's arm was still killing him. He was feeling so discouraged that he didn't even care about the final games of the World Series, which had been delayed by the earthquake.

Two days after he arrived home, Dave drove to Cleveland for a routine check on his arm. Dr.

Bergfield met with Jan and Dave to talk about the results of the MRI. He spoke very soberly and slowly, sometimes looking down at the ground. He told them both breaks seemed to be healing well. Then Dr. Bergfield stopped and put his head down. "But I'm not concerned about that right now. We really need to talk about these MRI results."

Dave and Jan knew something was wrong even before the doctor told them he couldn't be sure, but a new lump on Dave's arm looked exactly like a desmoid tumor. He was afraid the tumor had come back.

"Did you understand what the doctor was saying?" Jan asked as they drove home in the car after that appointment. "David, do you realize that he never mentioned your future in baseball, even once?"

Dave didn't respond right away because he didn't want to think about what Jan was saying. His whole life, he'd determined to play baseball no matter the odds. It had become an instinct for him. His motto, which he'd tacked up in his locker so he could see it every day, had been: *Never give up!*

"What are you going to do, David?" Jan wanted to know.

Dave tried to joke. "There you go again, writing me off."

"What would you say to me if I were in your shoes?" Jan demanded. "If I had cancer and wanted to continue with my career no matter what the risk, what would you say?"

Dave thought that was easy. "I'd tell you to quit, immediately. But Janice, you can't tell me what to do. I have to make this decision for myself."

That really made Jan mad. "Enough is enough!" she told Dave. "Would you risk your arm to throw that ball again? Is baseball that important?"

Dave didn't answer. He didn't see how he could quit.

As the days passed and he began thinking about retiring from baseball, he was surprised to find out that the thought began to bring him a sense of peace. He thought, *What more could I get from baseball that I haven't received already? Yes, I would miss the game, and I'd miss my friends. But why not quit?*

The following week the Draveckys flew back to California for some prior speaking engagements. When they got together with their friends the Hammakers, Dave told Atlee he had made the decision to retire from baseball.

"That's interesting," Atlee told him. "Bob Knepper called me yesterday and we talked about you. Bob said he was praying you would have peace about retiring from baseball.

"I couldn't pray that way for you," Atlee said. "I didn't know what you ought to do. I've just been praying that you would be at peace in whatever God led you to decide."

"I am, Atlee," Dave assured his friend. "It's as though a tremendous pressure has been released."

Dave's doctors had told him from the start that a desmoid tumor was hard to get rid of—that if a single cell were left, the tumor would grow back. And that's precisely what had happened.

So on January 4, 1990, Dave went back to Sloan-Kettering Hospital in New York City for a second operation. The surgeon cut away the cancer and sewed some thin plastic tubes into Dave's arm so that afterwards they could drop some pellets of radioactive iridium right down into the arm to kill any cancer cells that remained. The doctors were optimistic. Dave, however, tried to prepare for the worst while hoping for the best.

As it turned out, the operation was the beginning of a long, dark eighteen months for Dave. First, his arm wouldn't heal. The scar stayed raw. A little hole developed in it. Gradually, the hole got bigger until Dave could stick his finger down in it and tap the bone. His son Jonathan thought that was a neat trick, but the doctors did not.

Because of the hole, Dave went back for another operation in May. The doctor took a muscle out of his back and wrapped it around the bone. During that operation the surgeon made a troubling discovery. The tumor had come back and was growing near the radial nerve, crucial for controlling the hand. The doctors tried another form of radiation, but about the time Dave finished those treatments he came down with a serious staph infection in his arm.

"I was sick of being sick," Dave says. "I felt as if I'd been in a boxing ring with a lightweight punching me, and just about the time I was exhausted, the heavyweight came in to fight. Every time I turned around something new hit me in the face."

The antibiotics he got for the infection made Dave sick to his stomach. He'd get better for a while, and then the fever would flare up again. The worst of it was that his arm wouldn't heal. His fingers became numb. Dave began to doubt that his arm was going to get better.

In May of 1991 Dave went to New York for a regular three-month exam. The doctor examined him and then told Dave, "I think it's time."

"I knew instantly what he was talking about," Dave says. "It was time to cut off my arm."

12

ONE-ARMED MAN

Dave wasn't surprised or shocked by his doctor's suggestion. He'd been in and out of hospitals and had several operations, and his arm still wouldn't heal. It had become more and more of a nuisance over the past few months. So when the doctor suggested amputation, Dave simply looked at him and replied, "Okay. When do you want to do it?"

Jan and several family members and friends went with Dave when he checked into Sloan-Kettering Hospital in New York on June 17, 1991. After Dave got settled in his room, his dad started crying as he struggled to say what was on his heart. "I'm so tired of seeing you in so much pain, son, with that dead limb hanging from your body," he said. "Just get it off and be done with it."

Around noon the next day, Jan and Dave's parents hugged and kissed him as Dave was wheeled off to surgery. Then they waited. As the doctor expected, the cancer had come back a third time. He found it necessary to amputate part of Dave's shoulder as well, to make absolutely certain the tumor would never return. When Dave woke up that evening, Jan and Dave's mom stood at the foot of his bed and looked at him with obvious love and concern.

Dave didn't have a clear picture of what they were looking at until the following day. He forced himself out of bed so he could walk to the bathroom. That's where he saw himself for the first time after the surgery—in a small bathroom mirror. Dave stood there in his hospital gown, taking in the image that stared back at him—the reflection of a pale, one-armed man.

Dave was shocked at how radically the doctor had cut the arm back. The incision started at his neck and went diagonal to his underarm area. The arm was gone. The shoulder was gone. The shoulder blade was gone. Even the left side of his collarbone was gone.

"Okay, God," Dave prayed. "This is what I've got to live with. Put this behind me; let me go forward."

He remembers when the one-armed man in the mirror looked back at him. Dave says, "There was a peace in his eyes."

So many people sent flowers and candy that there wasn't room for them in Dave's room. Dave went around and shared his gifts with other people on his floor. Many of those patients were much sicker than Dave was, so he tried to express his faith and encourage them. Dave amazed everyone who knew him with how quickly he recovered after the amputation. The doctors had worried about him going into shock. Surprisingly, Dave actually felt better after the surgery than he had in a long time. During the six days he stayed in the hospital, he walked at least a mile a day. Not long after he got out of the hospital, he began giving interviews, answering letters, making public appearances, and even giving speeches.

On October 5, 1991, the Giants invited the Draveckys back to San Francisco for a special celebration: Dave Dravecky Day. He'd never been one for a lot of attention, but Dave felt honored by what the Giants wanted to do. Plus, he was excited about seeing old friends and returning to Candlestick Park one more time.

The entire Dravecky clan—Dave's folks, all his brothers and their families—plus a whole lot of friends, showed up in California for the occasion. The ballpark was packed for the final

Saturday afternoon game of the season against the rival Dodgers, who needed to win to go to the playoffs. So there was pre-game excitement in the air even before the Olympic theme music blasted out over the PA system and a throng of children and adults poured through the center field gates and spread over the field. High over their heads they carried banners and signs greeting Dave with such sentiments as:

Dave, Always a Giant
Dravecky #43
You Are a Giant Hero
Thanks for the Hope
Good Luck, Dave
God Bless U
Thanks for the Memories

The announcer's voice boomed over the crowd: "Faith, fortitude, and fearless determination in the face of adversity. Courage is Dave Dravecky."

As those words echoed through the stands, the fans stood and applauded as Dave, wearing a Giants uniform with number 43 on the back, walked out to a platform set up on the pitcher's mound. The Giants players followed him out of the dugout and onto the field where they sat on the infield grass alongside many of the Dodgers during a ceremony in which the Giants not only honored Dave, but gave out "Courageous Kid Awards" to five kids who had faced cancer with uncommon courage.

Then Dave stepped to the microphone and addressed the crowd. "God has allowed me to be a vehicle to help young kids like this. They are the real heroes—the five kids behind me." After the crowd applauded Dave continued, "I wish I could be on this mound today, but I can't. I want you to know, though, that putting on a Giants uniform meant more to me than anything in my professional career."

The huge screen in the outfield flashed the words "WE LOVE YOU, DAVE," as the crowd stood and cheered again.

"When I saw that," Dave said, "a rush of memories came back to me all at once, memories of when the words 'WELCOME BACK, DAVE' flashed across that same screen during my comeback game." He knew he would not be coming back this time, but he was taking the love of those fans with him forever.

Later, Dave wrote: "Tragedy pushes us through a one-way door, and once we pass through it, we can never return to the way life was before that tragedy. We can't go back, no matter how much we ache to do so. All we can do is give thanks for what once was for the happy times that were had, for the laughter, for the love, for the memories that were shared. Then saying good-bye to those times and to those loved ones, we can put our hand in the hand of him who gave orbit to the sun and the moon and the stars, and trust that he has a course for our lives as well."

Dave Dravecky really believed that. Because he did, and because he shared that faith with others, his faith inspired a lot of people across the country. His example and words encouraged many suffering from cancer and other problems. Because of that faith and his God-given determination, Dave made a remarkable adjustment to the loss of his left arm. He learned to write with his right hand. He fished with a device that holds the rod while he reeled in his catch. He took up swimming and weightlifting to stay in shape. What's more, he discovered that he enjoyed golf more than ever when he could play one-handed without feeling any pressure to be the best. "I could enjoy most of the activities I did before," Dave says, "if I was willing to take the time and work at it."

Yet, Dave was so concerned about the positive attitude he was projecting to those around him, so aware of the inspiration he was providing to thousands of people all over America, and so committed to making a strong and quick physical adjustment to his amputation that there was something important he didn't do: He never took the time to stop and face his own feelings of loss and grief. He downplayed his own natural emotions. When negative feelings eventually cropped up, he tried to ignore them because he didn't want, or know how, to talk about them with anyone else.

The truth was, Dave did have a huge emotional adjustment to make. Since the very first backyard games of catch with his dad, baseball had been his life. He admits, "It's what I watched on TV when I was indoors. It's what I played when I went outdoors. It's what I read about when I sprawled on the living room floor and spread out the Sunday paper.

"My life was wrapped up in baseball, and my life as a ballplayer was wrapped up in my arm. It wasn't long before my arm gained the attention of the neighborhood. When they chose sides for sandlot ball, I was the one they all wanted on their team for one reason—my arm.

"It wasn't long before that arm caught the attention of the entire school. My name started showing up on the sports page. Before long, I made headlines, all because of my arm.

"That arm attracted the attention of major-league scouts, and the part of me that was my boyhood became my livelihood. My ability to provide for my family didn't depend on my personality, how smart I was, or even how hard I worked.

It was based solely on what my arm could do on game day. The more strikes that arm could throw, the more I was worth. The more games that arm won, the more people wanted me on their team.

"Even when people talked with me, my arm was the center of conversation. 'How's the arm today, Dave?' 'Is your arm ready for tonight?' 'Better get some ice on that arm; don't want it to swell.'

"My arm was what people cheered me for, what they paid their hard-earned money to see. It's what made me valuable, what gave me worth, at least in the eyes of the world."

Suddenly, that arm was gone. How much of Dave Dravecky went with it? How much of what people thought of him went with it? Who was he going to be and what was he going to be like without it?

13

OUTREACH OF HOPE

As much as Dave Dravecky trusted God, there were a lot of questions he needed to answer, a number of issues he had to work through. For an independent athlete who always had been gifted in physical coordination, achievement, and control, it was especially frustrating to struggle with simple personal chores such as tucking in a shirttail or applying toothpaste to a toothbrush. Dave absolutely hated asking help for everything from cutting his meat at meals to tying the laces of his tennis shoes.

When he first retired, Dave didn't really miss baseball. After his arm was amputated, though, he started to miss everything about the sport—the feel of stitched seams on a new ball cradled in his hand, the smell of seasoned glove leather, the solid crack of a bat launching a line drive.

"Maybe it was a kind of phantom pain from the part of me that was severed," Dave says. "But I could feel a burning sensation where baseball had once been. I missed the competition and the relationships. Sometimes I felt the burning all the way down to my fingertips."

Those feelings gradually gave rise to many others. Frustration over his limitations. Fear that the cancer might come back. Worry about how Jan and his kids really felt about having a disfigured husband and father. Uncertainty about the future and what he might do for a living.

All this emotional baggage piled up inside and weighed him down until Dave not only began feeling physically ill, he became seriously depressed. He finally went to a doctor. This physician told Dave that he needed to honestly face his feelings, to open up and share them with others.

Dave still didn't know how to do that, until one morning when he felt particularly discouraged and disgusted with the pitiful-looking man he saw in the mirror. He turned to Jan and demanded, "How can you love me like this?"

"I'd love you if you didn't have *any* arms!" she assured him.

Not long after that, Dave finally opened up to Jan and let his feelings out. He told her about his fear of the cancer returning, about dying, and about her marrying someone else. He told her how frustrating it was to be dependent on other people, how painful it was to ask for help, how much he missed baseball, and how discouraged he sometimes got.

"Telling Jan all that," he says, "was hard for me to do. But after I did, it felt as if a huge weight was lifted from my shoulders."

At his next speaking engagement, Dave not only shared his inspiring testimony about how God had miraculously enabled him to come back from cancer to pitch again, but he openly and honestly talked about his continuing struggles and how he still needed to trust God to help him face those as well. Dave soon found that as he shared his deepest feelings and needs with Jan and some of his closest Christian friends, as he admitted his weaknesses to others, his load really did seem lighter. People weren't put off or disappointed in him. On the contrary, other people seemed freer to be open with him. It enriched and deepened relationships so that Dave could be encouraged, as well as encourage others.

From the beginning of his battle with cancer, Dave had realized God was using the experience in an incredible way to provide hope to others. He'd also become convinced that God was calling and preparing him to do some sort of ministry. So

Dave and Jan established The Dave Dravecky Foundation as a means of responding to the tens of thousands of cards and letters they received and to reach out to all those desperate and hurting people who wrote, called, and looked to them for encouragement and help.

Dave had been glad to accept a few of the countless speaking invitations to share his faith and to tell his amazing comeback story. He hadn't even minded making phone calls and hospital visits to cancer patients and their families who were in desperate need of faith and hope. Dave also looked forward to the day when the publicity and attention given to his personal battle against cancer would die down and he could get on to the next stage of his life, to whatever ministry God had in store for his future.

For a while, Dave thought God was calling him to minister to other professional baseball players. That seemed like a natural fit. He'd been a ballplayer, so he knew their needs. Plus, it would enable him to stay in touch with the game he loved. So to get a fresh start and to put some of the painful memories and times behind them, Dave, Jan, and their kids moved from Ohio to Colorado Springs with the idea of launching some sort of baseball ministry. Unfortunately, nothing happened. None of their plans seemed to be working out. None of their prayers seemed to be answered.

Dave became very discouraged again.

One day Jan came to him and said, "We've been looking and praying so hard for God to show us his plan. I think the answer has been right under our noses all along and we haven't wanted to admit it."

"What's that?" Dave asked.

Jan said, "I think we need to be encouraging cancer patients and amputees all over the country."

Dave looked at his wife and said, "That's crazy. I don't want to do that. That would remind me of my own pain and suffering every day."

At first, Jan didn't say anything. Then she looked at her husband and said, "Dave, where in the Bible does it say God wants to make us comfortable? Maybe he wants to get us out of our comfort zone and push us to the point of trusting him. So let's just trust him."

The more they thought and talked about it, the more Dave began to realize Jan was right. He had always believed God wanted to use his experience in some sort of ministry; he'd just assumed that meant his baseball experience. Perhaps the more valuable experience he had to share was what he'd learned through his pain and suffering. Maybe he could share encouragement and hope with the incredible number of people who continued to write and call to share their own stories of hurt and loss.

So that's what Jan and Dave set out to do.

The Dave Dravecky Foundation underwent a name change to become Dave Dravecky's Outreach of Hope. Jan and Dave both began looking for new ways they could comfort, encourage, and give hope to others who faced the same sort of struggles the Draveckys had known.

God has greatly blessed and multiplied Dave and Jan's ministry in the years since they began their Outreach of Hope. They constantly correspond and communicate the love of Jesus Christ to cancer patients and amputees in need of their personal encouragement. They also challenge, encourage, and train other Christians to respond as Christ did to people who are hurting. Dave and Jan work with health professionals around the country to provide resources for them and for their patients who are dealing with the emotional and spiritual aspects of living with cancer or amputation. They have created a nationwide ministry of prayer support for patients and their families because they believe in the importance of people connecting to God through prayer. They've also written a number of books and have created resources to help encourage others.

One of their biggest recent projects has been a special edition of the Bible designed especially for people who are hurting. The Draveckys and their friend, Joni Eareckson Tada, include personal notes and insights in *The Encouragement Bible*.

Dave says that the suffering people he encounters and whose stories he hears every day no longer remind him of his own pain and suffering. Instead, he says that God has shown him an invaluable lesson: The more he is able to help and encourage others, the more encouragement he receives from them himself.

Dave Dravecky still has a dream, but it's a new dream he wants to share. It's a dream of hope—God's message of hope. This beautiful message is summarized in an Outreach of Hope brochure quoting from the apostle Paul's second letter to the church in Corinth: "Therefore we do not lose heart. Though outwardly we are wasting away, yet inwardly we are being renewed day by day. For our light and momentary troubles are achieving for us an eternal glory that far outweighs them all. So we fix our eyes not on what is seen, but on what is unseen. For what is seen is temporary, but what is unseen is eternal" (2 Corinthians 4:16–18).

It's a great dream, farther reaching than what baseball could have afforded. It is a vision based on words from the very heart of God.

DISCOVER THE HERO IN YOU WITH TODAY'S HEROES BOOKS!

Written by Gregg & Deborah Shaw Lewis

Ben Carson
Softcover 0-310-70298-4

Colin Powell
Softcover 0-310-70299-2

David Robinson
Softcover 0-310-70297-6

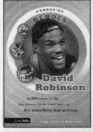

Joni Eareckson Tada
Softcover 0-310-70300-X

Brother Andrew
Softcover 0-310-70313-1

Dave Dravecky
Softcover 0-310-70314-X

Available now at your local bookstore!

Zonder**kidz**™

Grand Rapids, MI 49530
www.zonderkidz.com

We want to hear from you. Please send your comments about this book to us in care of the address below. Thank you.

Zonder**kidz**™

Grand Rapids, MI 49530
www.zonderkidz.com